DISCOVER PEACE

30-Day Devotion on Tried & Tested Scriptures

Nate Freeman

Veracity Academy

ISBN: 9798871569504

Cover design by: Art Painter
Library of Congress Control Number: 2018675309
Printed in the United States of America

CONTENTS

INTRODUCTION

In "Discovering Peace: A 30-Day Devotion on Tried and Tested Scriptures," we embark on a spiritual journey to deepen our understanding and experience of peace in the Christian walk. This book is not just a collection of daily devotions; it is an invitation to explore the profound peace that comes from a life rooted in Scripture and God's promises. In a world where chaos and uncertainty often prevail, the need for a steadfast, unshakeable peace has never been more pronounced. This devotional seeks to meet that need by guiding readers through a carefully curated selection of scriptures, each offering a unique perspective on peace as outlined in the Bible.

Each day of this devotional series presents a specific scripture accompanied by an observation, a personal application, and a prayer. These components are designed to provide a comprehensive approach to understanding and applying the principles of peace in everyday life. The scriptures have been chosen not only for their direct references to peace but also for their ability to speak to the diverse situations that require

God's peace. These scriptures provide a tried and tested foundation for cultivating lasting peace, from dealing with internal struggles and external conflicts to navigating life's uncertainties and embracing God's promises.

As we journey through these 30 days, we aim to move beyond a superficial understanding of peace as merely the absence of conflict or trouble. Instead, we delve into the biblical concept of peace as a profound sense of well-being and wholeness that emanates from a close relationship with God. This peace, often beyond human comprehension, is a gift from God, available to all who seek it through faith in Jesus Christ. It's our prayer that through "Discovering Peace," readers will not only encounter this divine peace in a fresh and transformative way but will also be equipped to live out this peace daily, becoming beacons of calm and assurance in a world desperately in need of the true peace that only God can provide.

DAY 1: THE FOUNDATION OF TRUE PEACE

Scripture:

John 14:27 (NLT) - "I am leaving you with a gift—peace of mind and heart. And the peace I give is a gift the world cannot give. So don't be troubled or afraid."

Observation:

In this passage, Jesus speaks to His disciples, offering them a parting gift - peace of mind and heart. This peace is distinctly different from what the world offers. It's not based on circumstances or human understanding; it's a deeper, more profound peace that comes only from Christ. Regardless of our situation, it reassures us not to be troubled or afraid.

3

Application:

Reflecting on my journey, I have encountered turmoil and uncertainty. It could have been easy to succumb to fear or anxiety. However, by clinging to this scripture, I've experienced the profound peace Jesus speaks of. This peace isn't an absence of trouble but a tranquil assurance in the midst of it. It reminds me that no matter what challenges I face - health, personal loss, or professional setbacks - there's a peace that transcends human understanding. Embracing this truth daily helps me not to be swayed by the transient troubles of the world but to remain anchored in Christ's unshakable peace.

Prayer:

Heavenly Father, I thank You for the gift of Your peace, which surpasses all understanding. In a world filled with turmoil and uncertainty, Your peace is a refuge for my soul. Help me remember that Your peace depends not on my circumstances but on Your unchanging nature. Teach me to trust in You, not to be troubled or afraid, no matter what I face. Guide me in Your ways, and let Your peace rule in my heart today and always in the name of Jesus. Amen.

DAY 2: FINDING PEACE IN CHAOS

Scripture:

Psalm 46:1-2 (NLT) - "God is our refuge and strength, always ready to help in times of trouble. So we will not fear when earthquakes come and the mountains crumble into the sea."

Observation:

These verses from Psalm 46 show a powerful contrast between the world's turmoil and God's steadfastness. The psalmist paints a picture of natural disasters and upheaval yet firmly declares trust in God as an unyielding source of refuge and peace. This scripture teaches us that even amidst the most incredible chaos, we can find unwavering peace in the presence and power of God. It's a testament to the kind of peace that isn't dependent on external calm but on a deep-seated trust in God's protective care.

Application:

Throughout my journey, I've encountered times when life felt as chaotic and unpredictable as an earthquake. In these moments of upheaval, where everything I knew seemed to be shifting, this passage has been a grounding force. It reminds me that peace doesn't come from the absence of trouble but from a conscious reliance on God's strength and protection. His presence offers a sanctuary of peace that can endure any storm. Embracing this truth allows me to face life's challenges not with fear but with a peaceful heart, confident in God's unceasing support and love.

Prayer:

Heavenly Father, I turn to You as my refuge and strength in the face of life's chaos and uncertainties. Remind me that no matter the turmoil, Your presence provides a peace that surpasses all understanding. Help me to anchor my heart in You, finding calm amidst the storms of life. Strengthen my faith and trust in Your constant care. May Your peace, which transcends all chaos, guard my heart and mind in the name of Jesus. Amen.

DAY 3: FINDING PEACE IN TRUST

Scripture:

Proverbs 3:5-6 (NLT) - "Trust in the LORD with all your heart; do not depend on your own understanding. Seek his will in all you do, and he will show you which path to take."

Observation:

These verses from Proverbs emphasize the importance of wholehearted trust in God. It advises against relying solely on our understanding, which can be limited and fallible. Instead, it encourages seeking God's will in every aspect of life. The promise is clear and profound: when we trust God and seek His guidance, He will direct our paths, leading us to the right decisions and courses of action.

Application:

In my walk with God, this scripture has been a cornerstone. There have been times when the way forward seemed unclear, and my understanding and reasoning felt inadequate. In these moments, leaning on this scripture has provided peace and clarity. Trusting God with all my heart means surrendering control, not leaning on my limited perspective, but seeking His will in every decision. This trust brings a sense of peace, knowing that God is guiding my steps, leading me on the right path even when I can't see the entire journey ahead.

Prayer:

Dear Lord, I come before You today with a heart seeking to trust You fully. I acknowledge that my understanding is limited, but Your wisdom is infinite. Help me to trust in You with all my heart and not to lean on my insights. In every decision and step I take, guide me according to Your will. Let Your peace fill my heart as I surrender my plans to You, trusting that You will lead me on the right path. Thank You for Your faithful guidance and unending love, in the name of Jesus, Amen.

DAY 4: THE PEACE OF GOD'S CONSTANT PRESENCE

Scripture:

Romans 8:38-39 (NLT) - "And I am convinced that nothing can ever separate us from God's love. Neither death nor life, neither angels nor demons, neither our fears for today nor our worries about tomorrow—not even the powers of hell can separate us from the love of God that is revealed in Christ Jesus our Lord."

Observation:

In this profound declaration from Romans, Paul speaks of the unbreakable bond between us and God's love, highlighting the eternal peace it offers.

This scripture reassures us that nothing can sever us from God's enduring love, regardless of life's trials and tribulations or even spiritual battles. It is a testament to the peace that comes from this certainty, a peace that persists in the face of life's greatest uncertainties and fears.

Application:

Reflecting on my life's journey, I recognize that peace does not stem from a life free of challenges but from the unwavering assurance of God's love. In times of doubt and fear, or when the future seems daunting, this scripture has been a beacon of peace, reminding me that God's love is a constant, unchanging force. It provides a sense of serenity and stability, knowing that no matter what I face, I am eternally held in the embrace of God's love. This understanding enables me to face life with a peaceful heart, anchored not in my circumstances but in the unshakable love of God.

Prayer:

Heavenly Father, I am deeply grateful for the peace that comes from the assurance of Your unending love. This constant love is my source of comfort and peace in a world of uncertainty and change. Help me remember that no matter my challenges, Your love remains steadfast and unbreakable. May this knowledge bring peace to my heart and mind, guiding me through every season of life, in the name of Jesus, whose love is our eternal anchor, Amen.

DAY 5: NAVIGATING LIFE WITH THE PEACE OF GOD'S WORD

Scripture:

Psalm 119:105 (NLT) - "Your word is a lamp to guide my feet and a light for my path."

Observation:

Psalm 119:105 poetically captures the role of God's Word as a guiding force in our lives. It's portrayed as both a lamp and a light, essential for navigating life's often dark and uncertain journey. This scripture emphasizes the peace that comes from having a reliable source of guidance and direction, particularly in moments of doubt or confusion.

Application:

This verse has been a source of tranquil assurance, especially in times of indecision or when the way forward is unclear. Turning to God's Word has consistently provided clarity and a sense of profound peace. It reassures me that I have a steadfast guide in the scriptures, even in the darkest and most uncertain times. This peace comes from knowing that I am not wandering but am being led along a path illuminated by God's wisdom and truth. Embracing God's Word as my guide ensures that I can navigate life with a peaceful and confident heart, no matter the situation.

Prayer:

Heavenly Father, thank You for the peace that Your Word brings into my life. Your scriptures are a source of light and direction in a world where the way forward can often seem clouded and uncertain. Guide me through Your Word, and let it be a lamp unto my feet, bringing peace to my journey. In every step I take, may Your Word illuminate my path and provide the calm assurance I need to move forward in Your will. In Jesus' name, Amen.

DAY 6: PEACE BEYOND CIRCUMSTANCES

Scripture:

Philippians 4:6-7 (NLT) - "Don't worry about anything; instead, pray about everything. Tell God what you need, and thank him for all he has done. Then you will experience God's peace, which exceeds anything we can understand. His peace will guard your hearts and minds as you live in Christ Jesus."

Observation:

In this passage, Paul provides a profound solution to anxiety and worry: prayer and gratitude. He encourages believers not to worry but to bring every concern to God in prayer and thanksgiving. The promise is striking – the peace of God, which surpasses all understanding, will guard our hearts and minds. This peace is not just a feeling; it's a divine guard, a protective shield provided by God Himself.

Application:

Reflecting on my own life, I've found that worry and anxiety often stem from focusing on problems rather than on God. This scripture reminds me that in every situation, I have the choice to either worry or to pray and give thanks. Choosing the latter has led me to experience God's incomprehensible peace that remains even in life's storms. It's a peace that doesn't necessarily change my circumstances but changes how I view and handle them. By turning my worries into prayers and cultivating a heart of gratitude, I find a peace that truly transcends human understanding, keeping my heart and mind secure in Christ.

Prayer:

Heavenly Father, I come to You today choosing to lay down my worries and anxieties at Your feet. In every circumstance, help me to turn to prayer and thanksgiving, trusting that You are in control. Thank You for the promise of Your peace that surpasses all understanding. Please guard my heart and mind with this peace as I navigate life's challenges. Teach me to rest in the assurance of Your care and to live each day in the tranquility of Your peace. In the name of Jesus, Amen.

DAY 7: ANCHORED IN CHRIST'S PEACE

Scripture:

Colossians 3:15 (NLT) - "And let the peace of Christ rule in your hearts, to which indeed you were called in one body. And be thankful."

Observation:

This verse from Colossians invites believers to let the peace of Christ take charge in their hearts. It's more than a suggestion. It's a directive to actively allow Christ's peace to govern our emotions, decisions, and responses. This peace is a hallmark of our calling as one body in Christ. The verse concludes with a call to gratitude, implying that thankfulness is intertwined with experiencing Christ's peace.

Application:

This verse is a powerful reminder of where my peace should originate in my spiritual walk. There are countless sources of stress and unrest in daily life, but the peace of Christ offers a different kind of tranquility—one that is not contingent on external circumstances. Allowing this peace to rule in my heart means consciously choosing Christ's way over anxiety or discord. It means letting His peace guide my decisions, interactions, and reactions. Whenever I feel overwhelmed, I recall this scripture, reminding myself to let Christ's peace be the anchor in my life and to approach each day with a heart full of gratitude.

Prayer:

Lord Jesus, I pray today to embrace the peace You offer fully. Help me to let Your peace rule in my heart, guiding my thoughts, words, and actions. Amid life's challenges and uncertainties, remind me that I am called to live in the peace You provide. Teach me to cultivate a spirit of gratitude, recognizing how it enriches and deepens the peace I experience. Thank You for Your unending peace, which provides a firm foundation in every aspect of my life. In Your holy name, Jesus, Amen.

DAY 8: LIVING IN HARMONY WITH OTHERS

Scripture:

Romans 12:18 (NLT) - "If it is possible, as far as it depends on you, live at peace with everyone."

Observation:

In this verse from Romans, Paul gives practical advice on living out the Christian faith in everyday relationships. The instruction is clear and proactive: make every effort to live peacefully with those around you. It acknowledges that while achieving peace may not always be possible (due to factors beyond our control), there is a personal responsibility to strive for harmony and peace in our interactions with others.

Application:

This scripture often comes to mind when I face conflicts or challenging relationships. It's a reminder that peace isn't just a state of mind; it's an active pursuit of how we relate to others. It challenges me to examine my actions and attitudes, ensuring I do my part to foster peace. This means sometimes extending forgiveness, choosing understanding over judgment, or being the first to seek reconciliation. Living out this verse isn't always easy, but it's vital to embodying Christ's teachings and fostering a peaceful community. It's about doing my part to create an environment where peace can thrive.

Prayer

Heavenly Father, I pray for the wisdom and grace to live peacefully with those around me. Help me to be an instrument of Your peace in my relationships, seeking harmony and understanding. Guide me in handling conflicts with love and patience, always striving to do my part in maintaining peace. Give me the strength to extend forgiveness and the humility to seek reconciliation when I am at fault. May my actions and words reflect Your love and contribute to a peaceful community. In Jesus' name, Amen.

DAY 9: THE PEACE IN GOD'S PRESENCE

Scripture:

Psalm 16:8- "I know the LORD is always with me. I will not be shaken, for he is right beside me."

Observation:

This verse from Psalm 16 emphasizes the stabilizing presence of God in our lives. The Psalmist expresses a deep sense of confidence and tranquility rooted in knowing that the Lord is always near. This proximity to God provides a foundation that prevents the believer from being shaken by life's uncertainties and challenges.

Application:

Reflecting on this scripture, I am reminded of

the countless times when God's presence brought immense peace to my heart. In moments of anxiety or facing daunting challenges, remembering that the Lord is always with me provides a profound sense of serenity. This assurance calms my fears, steadies my spirit, and gives me the strength to face whatever comes my way. It's a reminder that in God's presence, there is a peace that surpasses all understanding and keeps me grounded and unshaken amidst life's trials.

Prayer:

Dear Lord, thank You for the assurance of Your constant presence in my life. Knowing that You are always with me brings a wave of peace beyond measure. Help me to continually be aware of Your presence, especially in times of trouble or uncertainty. In Your presence, may I find the strength and serenity to face anything that comes my way. Let Your nearness be a constant source of peace and stability in my life. In the name of Jesus, I pray, Amen.

DAY 10: CULTIVATING PEACE THROUGH FORGIVENESS

Scripture:

Ephesians 4:31-32 (NLT) - "Get rid of all bitterness, rage, anger, harsh words, and slander, as well as all types of evil behavior. Instead, be kind to each other, tenderhearted, forgiving one another, just as God through Christ has forgiven you."

Observation:

These verses in Ephesians guide us towards shedding negative, harmful emotions and behaviors and instead embracing kindness, compassion, and forgiveness. This shift is not just about improving interpersonal relationships, but it's deeply rooted in the example of Christ's forgiveness towards us.

The call to forgive is tied to the transformative experience of having been forgiven by God through Christ.

Application:

In my own life, I have found that harboring bitterness and anger disrupts inner peace, not just with others but within myself. This scripture challenges me to reflect on the areas where I might need to let go of negative emotions and extend forgiveness. Embracing this teaching has been pivotal in cultivating a more profound sense of peace. It's a continual process of remembering how much Christ has forgiven me and allowing that grace to flow through me towards others. Forgiveness is not always easy, but it is a powerful pathway to peace, healing relationships, and restoring harmony in my heart and those around me.

Prayer:

Heavenly Father, thank You for the gift of forgiveness I received through Jesus Christ. Teach me to let go of bitterness, anger, and resentment and to embrace forgiveness and kindness. Help me to be tenderhearted, reflecting Your love and grace in my interactions with others. Guide me in the path of forgiveness, knowing it leads to true peace. May my heart mirror Yours in all that I do and say. In Jesus' name, Amen.

DAY 11: PEACE THROUGH TRUSTING GOD'S TIMING

Scripture:

Ecclesiastes 3:1, 11(NLT)- "For everything there is a season, a time for every activity under heaven. ... Yet God has made everything beautiful in its own time. He has planted eternity in the human heart, but even so, people cannot see the whole scope of God's work from beginning to end."

Observation:

These verses from Ecclesiastes speak to the divine timing and order in our lives. They remind us that every aspect of our existence has its appointed time and that God works through these seasons to bring beauty and purpose. The passage acknowledges our human limitation in fully understanding God's timing, yet it invites us to trust in His perfect plan.

Application:

In moments of impatience or frustration, when things don't seem to be happening as quickly as I would like, this scripture brings me back to peace. It reminds me that God's timing is not my timing, and His ways are not my ways. Trusting in God's timing means surrendering my plans and understanding and believing He will make all things beautiful in their time. This trust brings a sense of peace, freeing me from anxiety over the future and allowing me to live fully in the present, knowing that God is in control.

Prayer:

Lord God, I thank You for the reminder that there is a season for everything under heaven. Help me to trust in Your timing, knowing that You make all things beautiful in their time. When I become impatient or anxious about the future, remind me to rest in Your perfect plan. Grant me the peace that comes from trusting in Your sovereignty over every aspect of my life. Teach me to embrace the journey, with its various seasons, as part of Your divine design. In Jesus' name, Amen.

DAY 12: THE STRENGTH OF PEACEFUL ENDURANCE

Scripture:

James 1:2-4(NLT) - "Dear brothers and sisters, when troubles of any kind come your way, consider it an opportunity for great joy. For you know that when your faith is tested, your endurance has a chance to grow. So let it grow, for when your endurance is fully developed, you will be perfect and complete, needing nothing."

Observation:

This passage from James offers a counterintuitive perspective on facing trials: seeing them as opportunities for joy. The testing of faith through various challenges is seen not as a setback but a means to develop endurance. This endurance is key to spiritual maturity and completeness. It implies a peaceful resilience that can withstand life's storms.

Application:

In my life, like many others, trials, and challenges have often seemed overwhelming. Yet, this scripture has encouraged me to view these difficulties through a different lens – as opportunities for growth and strengthening of faith. It's about finding peace in trials, not by avoiding them but by enduring through them with a steadfast heart. This perspective shift doesn't minimize the pain or difficulty of the trials but offers a way to navigate them with a sense of peace and purpose. Embracing this approach has helped me develop a resilience grounded in faith and peace, regardless of the circumstances.

Prayer:

Heavenly Father, I come to You in times of trouble, seeking relief and the strength to endure. Help me to view my trials as opportunities to grow in faith and resilience. Grant me the peace from a deep trust in You, even in life's storms. Let my endurance be a testament to Your sustaining power and love. May I emerge from every challenge more mature, complete in You, and equipped to face whatever lies ahead. In the precious name of Jesus, Amen.

DAY 13: PEACE IN SURRENDERING CONTROL

Scripture:

Proverbs 16:9 (NLT) - "We can make our plans, but the LORD determines our steps."

Observation:

This verse from Proverbs highlights the human tendency to plan and control, juxtaposed with the ultimate sovereignty of God. It acknowledges our ability and need to make plans but gently reminds us that God guides and determines the outcome. This verse offers a profound sense of peace in recognizing and surrendering to God's greater wisdom and control.

Application:

In my own experience, the desire to control outcomes and orchestrate every detail of life can be a significant source of stress and anxiety. This scripture has been a calming reminder that, while it is wise to plan, ultimate control rests with the Lord. Surrendering to His will brings a liberating peace. It shifts the focus from my limited understanding to God's all-encompassing wisdom. This surrender doesn't mean passivity but rather aligning my plans with God's will and trusting in His guidance. It's a daily practice of letting go and finding peace in the assurance that God is directing my path.

Prayer:

Dear Heavenly Father, I acknowledge that while I make plans, You direct my steps. Help me surrender my need for control and trust in Your perfect guidance and timing. In moments of uncertainty and decision-making, remind me to seek Your will above my own. Grant me the peace that comes from trusting in Your sovereignty and wisdom. May I rest in knowing that You are orchestrating my life for good, even in ways I may not yet understand. In Jesus' name, Amen.

DAY 14: PEACE THROUGH RESTING IN GOD

Scripture::

Matthew 11:28-30 (NLT) - "Come to me, all of you who are weary and carry heavy burdens, and I will give you rest. Take my yoke upon you. Let me teach you, because I am humble and gentle at heart, and you will find rest for your souls. For my yoke is easy to bear, and the burden I give you is light."

Observation:

In these comforting words of Jesus, there is an open invitation to all who are burdened and weary. He offers rest, not as the world gives, but a deeper, soulful rest. This rest comes from taking up His yoke, a metaphor for joining in partnership with Him, learning from His gentle and humble heart. This passage speaks of a peace that comes from aligning ourselves with Christ and His way of life, which is inherently more restful and fulfilling than the heavy burdens we often carry on our own.

Application:

Throughout my journey, there have been times of weariness and heavy burdens where this scripture has been a source of immense comfort and peace. It reminds me that I don't have to carry my burdens alone. Turning to Jesus and taking on His yoke means sharing the load with Him and learning His ways of humility and gentleness. This brings a kind of peace different from mere relaxation or a break from activity. It's a peace that permeates the soul, offering rest and renewal. Embracing this truth helps me to cast my cares upon Him regularly and find a peaceful rest that rejuvenates my spirit.

Prayer:

Lord Jesus, I come to You today, weary and burdened, seeking the rest that only You can provide. Teach me to take Your yoke upon me and to learn from Your humble and gentle heart. Help me to find true rest and peace for my soul in You. Lighten my burdens as I share them with You, and guide me in Your ways of peace and rest. Thank You for the promise of a lighter load and a peaceful heart in partnership with You. In Jesus' name, Amen.

DAY 15: PEACE IN GOD'S PROTECTIVE CARE

Scripture:

Psalm 91:1-2 (NLT) - "Those who live in the shelter of the Most High will find rest in the shadow of the Almighty. This I declare about the Lord: He alone is my refuge, my place of safety; He is my God, and I trust Him."

Observation:

These opening verses of Psalm 91 paint a vivid picture of divine protection and peace. The imagery of living in God's shelter and resting in His shadow conveys a sense of security and tranquility. It's a declaration of trust in God as a refuge and haven, emphasizing the peace from being in His protective care.

Application:

This scripture resonates deeply with me, especially when the world feels unsafe or uncertain. It reminds me that true safety and peace are found in God's presence. By choosing to dwell in the 'shelter of the Most High,' I am consciously deciding to place my trust and security in God rather than in worldly assurances. This decision brings profound peace, knowing I am under the care of the Almighty, whose protection is unparalleled. It's a daily reminder to seek refuge in God's presence, where I find rest and peace for my soul.

Prayer:

Almighty God, I thank You for the promise of Your protection and peace. Help me to live in the shelter of Your presence, finding rest and safety in Your shadow. You are my refuge and my strength, the source of my peace in a turbulent world. Teach me to trust You more deeply, to rest in the assurance of Your care and protection. May Your peace, which surpasses all understanding, guard my heart and mind as I abide in You. In the name of Jesus, I pray, Amen.

DAY 16: PEACE THROUGH FAITH AMIDST UNCERTAINTY

Scripture:

Hebrews 11:1(NLT) - "Faith shows the reality of what we hope for; it is the evidence of things we cannot see."

Observation:

This profound verse from Hebrews defines faith as the assurance and conviction of things not seen. It speaks to the idea that faith bridges the gap between our present reality and our hopes for the future. In the context of peace, this verse suggests that peace comes from trusting in God's promises and His unseen work, even when our current circumstances might seem unstable or uncertain.

Application:

There have been numerous instances where the future seemed unclear and my path needed to be made clearer. This scripture has been a cornerstone in these moments, reminding me that faith is not about having clarity in every detail but about trusting in God's sovereignty and goodness. It's about finding peace amid uncertainty, not by seeing but by believing. Faith in God's promises and His character brings peace that calms anxiety and fear, allowing me to walk confidently even when I cannot see the road ahead.

Prayer:

Heavenly Father, thank You for the gift of faith that bridges the gap between my present circumstances and Your eternal promises. In times of uncertainty and doubt, strengthen my faith. Help me to find peace in trusting You, even when I cannot see the outcome. May my faith be the evidence of Your work in my life and the assurance of my hope in You. Grant me the serenity of trusting in Your unseen guidance and providential care. In the precious name of Jesus, Amen.

DAY 17: PEACE IN LETTING GO OF WORRY

Scripture:

Matthew 6:34 (NLT) - "So don't worry about tomorrow, for tomorrow will bring its own worries. Today's trouble is enough for today."

Observation:

In this teaching, Jesus addresses the human tendency to worry about the future. He advises focusing on the present and not being consumed by concerns about what may happen tomorrow. This perspective encourages a peaceful approach to life, one that trusts in God's care and provision and focuses on dealing with the present moment rather than being overwhelmed by future uncertainties.

Application:

This verse has often served as a gentle reminder to me not to get caught up in future anxieties. It's easy to become preoccupied with 'what ifs' and potential problems that may never materialize. Jesus' words here invite me to a state of peace, grounded in the present and trusting in God's handling of the future. Focusing on today and relinquishing my worries about tomorrow gives me a greater sense of calm and trust in God's plan. This approach doesn't mean being irresponsible about the future but choosing not to let worries about what hasn't happened yet disrupt my peace today.

Prayer:

Lord Jesus, thank You for Your wise counsel to not worry about tomorrow. Help me to trust in Your providence and care, focusing on the present and leaving the future in Your capable hands. Teach me to find peace in the midst of today's challenges without being burdened by the worries of tomorrow. May Your peace, which surpasses all understanding, guard my heart and mind as I learn to live fully in each moment You have given me. In Jesus' name, I pray, Amen.

DAY 18: PEACE DURING CONFLICT

Scripture:

Matthew 5:9 (NLT) - "Blessed are the peacemakers, for they will be called children of God."

Observation:

This verse is one of the Beatitudes spoken by Jesus, highlighting the value and blessing of being a peacemaker. It implies that peace is not just a state to be enjoyed, but also a role to be actively pursued. Being a peacemaker involves seeking resolution and harmony in situations of conflict. This pursuit aligns with the character of God, and those who engage in it are recognized as His children.

Application:

In my personal and professional life, conflicts inevitably arise. This scripture reminds me that my response to these situations should reflect my identity as a child of God. Seeking peace does not mean avoiding conflict but approaching disagreements with a heart geared toward reconciliation and understanding. Being a peacemaker often requires patience, humility, and wisdom. It's a proactive choice to create an atmosphere of harmony and understanding, even in challenging circumstances. Living out this principle has brought a deeper sense of peace to my relationships, knowing that I am embodying a core aspect of my faith in seeking peace.

Prayer:

Heavenly Father, I seek Your wisdom and guidance to be a peacemaker in my daily interactions. Help me to approach conflicts with a heart intent on reconciliation and understanding. Grant me the patience, humility, and wisdom needed to navigate difficult situations and to bring peace where there is discord. Let my life reflect Your love and peace so I may truly be called Your child. In Jesus' name, I pray for the grace to be a source of peace in a world that often seems divided. In the name of Jesus. Amen.

DAY 19: PEACE IN CHOOSING CONTENTMENT

Scripture:

Philippians 4:11-12(NLT) - "Not that I was ever in need, for I have learned how to be content with whatever I have. I know how to live on almost nothing or with everything. I have learned the secret of living in every situation, whether it is with a full stomach or empty, with plenty or little."

Observation:

In these verses, the Apostle Paul speaks about the virtue of contentment. He has learned to be content in every situation, whether in abundance or need. This contentment is not dependent on external circumstances but a state of peace and satisfaction from within. Paul's words suggest that peace is closely tied to our attitude toward our circumstances rather than the circumstances themselves.

Application:

Reflecting on my own life, there have been times of abundance and periods of scarcity. This scripture has taught me that true peace does not come from material possessions or favorable circumstances but from a state of contentment with whatever I have. Learning to be content in all situations is a powerful way to cultivate inner peace. It involves a conscious decision to focus on the blessings present in each moment and to trust in God's provision, regardless of what I may or may not have. Embracing contentment as a lifestyle choice leads to a more peaceful and fulfilling life.

Prayer:

Dear Lord, thank You for the Apostle Paul's example of contentment in all circumstances. Teach me to find contentment and peace in whatever situation I am in, knowing that my happiness and peace depend not on external factors but on my relationship with You. Help me appreciate what I have and trust in Your provision in times of need. Cultivate in me a heart of gratitude and contentment that I may experience the true peace that comes from a life lived in harmony with Your will. In Jesus' name, Amen.

DAY 20: PEACE THROUGH SERVING OTHERS

Scripture:

Galatians 5:13-14(NLT) - "For you have been called to live in freedom, my brothers and sisters. But don't use your freedom to satisfy your sinful nature; instead, use your freedom to serve one another in love. For the whole law can be summed up in this one command: 'Love your neighbor as yourself.'"

Observation:

In this passage, Paul emphasizes the dual nature of Christian freedom. While believers are freed from the constraints of sin and the law, this freedom is not meant for self-indulgence. Rather, it's an opportunity to serve others in love, reflecting the core Christian principle of loving one's neighbor as oneself. This service is not just an act of obedience but a path to a deeper, more fulfilling peace that comes from selfless love and community.

Application:

In my own life, serving others has often been a source of peace and fulfillment. This scripture reminds me that my actions towards others should not be about fulfilling my desires but loving and serving them as I would. It shifts the focus from a self-centered view to a community-centered one. In practicing this, I've found a profound sense of peace and purpose, knowing that my actions are contributing to the well-being of others and aligning with God's will. Serving others in love becomes not just a duty but a joyful expression of my freedom in Christ.

Prayer:

Gracious God, thank You for the freedom I have in Christ. Help me to use this freedom not for personal gain but as an opportunity to serve others in love. Guide me to see and meet the needs of those around me, loving my neighbor as myself. In serving others, may I find the deep peace that comes from selfless love and obedience to Your will. Teach me to cherish and embody the principle of loving service as a reflection of Your love for us all, in the name of Jesus, Amen.

DAY 21: PEACE IN THE ASSURANCE OF SALVATION

Scripture:

Romans 5:1(NLT) - "Therefore, since we have been made right in God's sight by faith, we have peace with God because of what Jesus Christ our Lord has done for us."

Observation:

In this powerful verse from Romans, The Apostle Paul speaks about the peace that comes from being justified by faith. This justification, or being made right with God, is not based on our efforts or righteousness but solely on what Jesus Christ has done. The peace mentioned here is profound, as it signifies a reconciled relationship with God, free from the hostility caused by sin.

Application:

Reflecting on this verse, I am reminded of the deep sense of peace that comes from knowing I am saved and reconciled with God through faith in Jesus Christ. This is not a peace that the world can give or take away; it's a peace that transcends understanding, rooted in the assurance of salvation. It liberates from the fear of judgment and fills the heart with gratitude for the unmerited grace received through Christ. This assurance transforms how I live, grounding my faith and giving me a calm assurance in the face of life's uncertainties and challenges.

Prayer:

Heavenly Father, I am deeply grateful for the peace that comes from being justified by faith in Jesus Christ. Thank you for the assurance of salvation and the reconciliation it brings with You. Help me to live daily in the light of this peace, letting it guide my thoughts, words, and actions. May this assurance shape my life, giving me a firm foundation. In Jesus' name, I celebrate and hold dear the peace from Your grace and love. Amen.

DAY 22: PEACE THROUGH TRUSTING IN GOD'S SOVEREIGNTY

Scripture:

Isaiah 26:3(NLT) - "You will keep in perfect peace all who trust in you, all whose thoughts are fixed on you!"

Observation:

This verse from Isaiah emphasizes the relationship between trust in God and peace. The promise is clear and powerful: those who trust in God and focus their thoughts on Him will be kept in perfect peace. This peace is tied to recognizing God's sovereignty and the trust that He is in control, even when circumstances suggest otherwise.

Application:

Throughout various stages of my life, I have encountered situations that seemed out of my control, causing anxiety and unrest. This scripture has often been a source of comfort and strength, reminding me that peace comes from fixing my thoughts on God and trusting in His sovereignty. It's about shifting my focus from the problems and uncertainties of life to the unchanging, all-powerful nature of God. This trust doesn't mean that challenges won't come, but it does mean that I can face them with peace grounded in the assurance of God's perfect control and care for my life.

Prayer:

Lord, I thank You for the promise of perfect peace that comes from trusting in You. Help me to fix my thoughts on You, especially in times of uncertainty and stress. Teach me to rely on Your sovereignty, knowing You control every aspect of my life. In life's storms, may Your peace, which surpasses all understanding, guard my heart and mind. I choose to trust You, confident in Your unfailing love and power. In the name of Jesus Christ, I pray, Amen.

DAY 23: PEACE DURING CHANGE

Scripture:

Hebrews 13:8(NLT) - "Jesus Christ is the same yesterday, today, and forever."

Observation:

This verse from Hebrews offers a profound truth about Jesus Christ: His unchanging nature. In a constantly evolving and often unpredictable world, this scripture provides a source of stability and peace. It reminds us that no matter what life changes we face, Jesus remains steadfast, reliable, and ever-present.

Application:

In my life, like many others, change has been a constant. Whether it's shifts in personal circumstances, transitions in work, or even broader societal changes, these shifts can sometimes bring uncertainty and unrest. This scripture, however, has been a bedrock of peace, reminding me that despite the flux of life, Jesus' character and promises remain unchanged. Knowing I can always rely on His unshakable presence and guidance brings comfort and stability. In times of change, this knowledge allows me to maintain a sense of peace rooted not in my circumstances but in the eternal constancy of Christ.

Prayer:

Lord Jesus, thank You for being the same yesterday, today, and forever. In a world of constant change, Your unchanging nature is a source of immense peace and comfort. Help me keep my eyes fixed on You, especially during transition and uncertainty. Remind me that you remain constant and faithful no matter what changes around me. May this truth anchor my heart in peace, regardless of life's shifting sands. In the name of Jesus, I pray, Amen.

DAY 24: PEACE THROUGH GOD'S GUIDANCE

Scripture:

Psalm 32:8(NLT) - "The Lord says, 'I will guide you along the best pathway for your life. I will advise you and watch over you.'"

Observation:

In this verse, God promises to provide guidance and counsel. It's a declaration of His active involvement in our lives, offering direction and oversight. This guidance is not generic but tailored to the best pathway for each individual. The peace in this scripture comes from knowing that God is not just a distant observer but an active guide and protector in our life's journey.

Application:

Throughout my life, making decisions, big or small, has often been a source of anxiety and uncertainty. This verse has been a comforting reminder that I am not alone in navigating life's complexities. God's promise to guide and advise offers peace and security. It means that I can rely on His wisdom and insight for my path rather than solely on my own understanding. This assurance helps to alleviate the stress of decision-making, knowing that God is with me, guiding each step according to His perfect plan.

Prayer:

Heavenly Father, thank You for Your promise to guide and watch over me. I seek Your wisdom and direction in all aspects of my life. Help me to listen for Your voice and to follow Your guidance with trust and obedience. In moments of uncertainty or decision, remind me that You are with me, offering Your counsel and leading the way. May Your peace fill my heart as I rely on Your guidance, knowing that You are directing me along the best pathway for my life, in the name of Jesus, Amen.

DAY 25: PEACE IN GOD'S UNCHANGING PROMISES

Scripture:

2 Corinthians 1:20 (NLT) - "For all of God's promises have been fulfilled in Christ with a resounding 'Yes!' And through Christ, our 'Amen' (which means 'Yes') ascends to God for his glory."

Observation:

This verse from 2 Corinthians highlights the reliability and fulfillment of God's promises in Christ. It affirms that every promise made by God finds its confirmation and fulfillment in Jesus. This assurance provides a foundation of peace, knowing that God's commitments are not wavering or uncertain but are made sure in Christ.

Application:

My faith journey has had moments of doubt and uncertainty, especially during challenging times. This scripture reassures me that the promises of God are steadfast and trustworthy. Whether it's the promise of God's presence, provision, or salvation, I can rest in the peace that these promises are already affirmed in Christ. This knowledge strengthens my faith and offers a sense of tranquility, understanding that God's word is unchanging and His promises are a sure foundation in a world that is often unstable and unpredictable.

Prayer:

Lord God, I thank You for the assurance of Your promises, all fulfilled in Christ. Help me trust these promises and find peace in their certainty and fulfillment. May my faith in Your word be strengthened, and may my life reflect the glory of Your promises realized in Jesus. As I hold onto Your promises, let Your peace, which surpasses all understanding, reign in my heart and mind. In the name of Jesus,, Amen.

DAY 26: PEACE IN GOD'S PLAN FOR THE FUTURE

Scripture:

Jeremiah 29:11(NLT) - "For I know the plans I have for you," says the LORD. "They are plans for good and not for disaster, to give you a future and a hope."

Observation:

This well-known verse from Jeremiah offers a powerful assurance of God's benevolent plans for His people. It speaks of plans not aimed at harm but at providing a hopeful and positive future. This promise is a source of peace, especially in times of uncertainty or hardship, as it reassures us of God's good intentions and sovereign control over our lives.

Application:

This scripture has been a cornerstone of hope and peace in various phases of my life, particularly during periods of change or difficulty. It reminds me that even when I cannot see the path ahead, God has a plan for my life for my good. This reassurance allows me to face the future with calm and trust rather than fear or anxiety. It encourages me to look beyond my current circumstances and trust in God's overarching plan, which is designed for my welfare and includes a hope-filled future.

Prayer:

Heavenly Father, I am grateful for Your promise of a hopeful future. In times of uncertainty and worry, help me to remember that Your plans for me are for good. Guide me in Your path and reassure me with the peace that comes from knowing You are in control. May I trust in Your loving purposes for my life, finding solace in Your plans always aimed at my well-being and hope. Thank You for Your constant care and guidance, in the name of Jesus, Amen.

DAY 27: PEACE IN SURRENDERING TO GOD'S WILL

Scripture:

Psalm 46:10 (NLT) - "Be still, and know that I am God! I will be honored by every nation. I will be honored throughout the world."

Observation:

This verse from Psalm 46 is a command for stillness and recognition of God's sovereignty. It invites us to pause, let go of our striving, and acknowledge God's supreme authority and power. The phrase "be still" is not just about physical stillness but also about ceasing to fret and worry and surrendering control to God. This surrender brings peace, knowing that God is in charge and His majesty will be recognized globally.

Application:

In my life, amidst the busyness and challenges, finding time to 'be still' can often seem difficult. Yet, this verse is a gentle but powerful reminder of the peace from surrendering to God's will. It reminds me to pause, reflect, and acknowledge God's control over my life and the world. This recognition helps to alleviate stress and anxiety, replacing them with a sense of calm and trust in God's plan. It's a reminder that peace comes not from managing every aspect of life alone but from knowing that God is in control.

Prayer:

Lord, in life's busyness and challenges, help me to find moments to be still and recognize Your sovereignty. Teach me to surrender my worries and plans to You and to trust in Your perfect will. May Your peace, which comes from this surrender, fill my heart. I acknowledge Your majesty and control over all things and choose to find rest in Your unchanging nature. Be glorified in my life and worldwide, in the name of Jesus, Amen.

DAY 28: PEACE THROUGH PRAYERFUL DEPENDENCE ON GOD

Scripture:

Philippians 4:6-7 (NLT) - "Don't worry about anything; instead, pray about everything. Tell God what you need, and thank him for all he has done. Then you will experience God's peace, which exceeds anything we can understand. His peace will guard your hearts and minds as you live in Christ Jesus."

Observation:

This passage from Philippians is a direct instruction

to replace worry with prayer. It encourages an open dialogue with God about our needs and a heart of gratitude for His past provisions. The promise is profound: by turning to prayer, we can experience God's peace, which is beyond human comprehension. This peace is not just a fleeting emotion; it guards our hearts and minds, providing stability and tranquility in Christ.

Application:

In times of stress and anxiety, I have often found solace in this scripture. It reminds me that instead of succumbing to worry, I have the powerful tool of prayer. By bringing my concerns and needs to God in prayer and remembering to thank Him for His faithfulness, I open my heart to His peace. This peace is transformative; it calms anxiety and provides a perspective transcending my immediate concerns. Practicing this prayerful dependence on God has been a key to experiencing a deep, abiding peace in various situations.

Prayer:

Heavenly Father, I choose to lay my worries before You in prayer. In every situation, help me turn to You with my needs and offer thanks for Your constant presence and provision. I welcome Your peace that surpasses all understanding to guard my heart and mind in Christ Jesus. May this peace guide me through life's ups and downs, keeping me anchored in Your love and care. In the precious name of Jesus, Amen.

DAY 29: PEACE IN EMBRACING GOD'S GRACE

Scripture:

Ephesians 2:14 (NLT) - "For Christ himself has brought peace to us. He united Jews and Gentiles into one people when, in his own body on the cross, he broke down the wall of hostility that separated us."

Observation:

This verse from Ephesians speaks to the profound peace that Christ has brought through His sacrifice. It emphasizes how His actions on the cross have reconciled humanity to God and broken down divisions among people, uniting them as one. This peace results from grace, transcending human efforts or merits and fostering unity and reconciliation.

Application:

Reflecting on this scripture, I am reminded of the incredible peace that comes from understanding and accepting Christ's grace. It's a peace that heals divisions, whether internal conflicts within myself or relational rifts with others. Recognizing that Christ has broken down these walls through His sacrifice encourages me to live in harmony and peace with those around me, embracing the unity His grace offers. This understanding helps cultivate a spirit of forgiveness, acceptance, and peace in my spiritual walk and interactions with others.

Prayer:

Lord Jesus, thank You for the peace You have brought through Your sacrifice on the cross. Help me to embrace the grace You offer, allowing it to break down walls of division and hostility in my life. Teach me to live in the unity and peace that Your grace makes possible, extending the same forgiveness and acceptance to others You have given me. May my life reflect the reconciliation and peace that is found in You. In Your holy name, Jesus, I pray, Amen.

DAY 30: PEACE IN THE ASSURANCE OF GOD'S LOVE

Scripture:

Romans 8:38-39 (NLT) - "And I am convinced that nothing can ever separate us from God's love. Neither death nor life, neither angels nor demons, neither our fears for today nor our worries about tomorrow—not even the powers of hell can separate us from the love of God that is revealed in Christ Jesus our Lord."

Observation:

This powerful declaration by Paul in Romans speaks to the unbreakable bond of God's love for us in Christ Jesus. It assures believers that nothing in existence can sever our connection to God's love. This encompasses all realms of existence, fears, worries, and even supernatural powers. The peace in this scripture comes from the certainty of God's unwavering, unfailing love.

Application:

In moments of doubt fear, or when I feel overwhelmed by life's challenges, this scripture serves as a profound reminder of the steadfast love of God. Knowing nothing can separate me from His love brings an immense sense of peace. This isn't peace based on circumstances or my performance but on the unchangeable nature of God's love. It encourages me to face each day with confidence, knowing that no matter what comes my way, I am enveloped in the security of God's love, a love that is both my shield and comfort.

Prayer:

Heavenly Father, I am grateful for the assurance of Your unending love. Thank You that nothing can separate me from Your love in Christ Jesus. In times of uncertainty fear, or when I feel overwhelmed, reminds me of this great truth. Let the knowledge of Your unfailing love be a source of unshakable peace in my life. No matter what I face today or in the future, I rest in peace from Your eternal, unchanging love. In the name of Jesus, Amen.

ABOUT THE AUTHOR: NATE FREEMAN

Nate Freeman is not just an author but a living testament to the transformative power of faith, resilience, and grace. His life story is an extraordinary tapestry of miracles and triumphs over staggering odds—making him uniquely qualified to inspire, motivate, and uplift others.

Early Life And Miracles

From surviving a diabetic coma at the tender age of 2, Nate has always been a fighter. His early life was marked by divine interventions and miracles that set the stage for a journey filled with purpose and meaning.

Health Triumphs

As an adult, Nate faced another life-threatening challenge: kidney failure. Thanks to a miraculous kidney and pancreas transplant, he was granted a new lease on life, reiterating his steadfast belief in the power of faith to surmount even the most insurmountable odds.

A Journey From Darkness to Light
In a twist of fate that could only be described as miraculous, Nate lost his sight during an eye surgery, only to regain it later. This profound experience has given him a unique perspective on life's challenges and the beauty of second chances.

Career And Advocacy

Over 30 years, Nate has honed his skills as a professional public speaker, captivating audiences from corporate professionals to non-profit organizations, educational institutions, and religious gatherings. His advocacy work is equally impactful—he led a national initiative focused on homelessness that secured an $8 million congressional appropriation. This real-world activism solidifies his status as an orator and a man of action.

Global Reach

Nate's influence transcends borders. With a social media following of over 300,000 and a globally-broadcasted television program, "Authenticity," his message of faith and transformation resonates globally.

Universal Appeal

Nate's ability to connect with individuals from all walks of life makes Nate most relatable. His diverse life experiences have molded him into a versatile messenger, capable of touching hearts and changing lives across a broad societal spectrum.

Through his writings, Nate Freeman continues to be a beacon of hope and empowerment, providing readers a compelling narrative and the tools to transform their lives through faith and action.

Contact Nate for speaking engagements, interviews, or collaboration opportunities. Your life may never be the same again.

https://asknatefreeman.com

nate@asknatefreeman.com

BOOKS BY THIS AUTHOR

A Grateful Heart: Daily Devotion For A Thankful Heart

Dive into the transformative journey of 'A Grateful Heart,' a Christian daily devotional that speaks to both the heart and soul. Whether you're a man or a woman, this scripture-based devotional offers 30 days of inspirational reflections, guiding you closer to spiritual growth and understanding. Each entry, crafted with eloquence by Nate Freeman, serves as a beacon of hope and gratitude, making it a perfect devotional for couples looking to grow together in faith. Accompanied by reflection questions, this devotional journal not only feeds the spirit but also encourages introspection and personal growth. Tailored for those seeking a deeper, guided devotional experience, 'A Grateful Heart' ensures every day is infused with prayer, inspiration, and a renewed sense of God's enduring love. Ideal for teens and adults alike, this is a devotional that transcends age, nurturing a prayerful heart brimming with gratitude.

From Gloom To Glory: Finding Joy Through Jesus Christ In The Midst Of Darkness

Discover the Unstoppable Power of Faith and Joy in the Midst of Life's Darkest Moments

In "From Gloom to Glory," author Nate Freeman offers an inspiring, soul-stirring journey through the valleys of despair to the mountaintops of joy and redemption. This book is not just a read; it's an experience, a journey alongside someone who has walked the treacherous paths of life's most daunting challenges and emerged with a message of hope and triumph. Nate's story is a testament to the unyielding strength found in faith in Jesus Christ, a beacon for anyone navigating through their own dark nights.